Once Around Is All You Get

Once Around Is All You Get

James F. Lichtman

Writers Club Press
San Jose New York Lincoln Shanghai

Once Around Is All You Get

Writers Club Press
an imprint of iUniverse.com, Inc.

For information address:
iUniverse.com, Inc.
5220 S 16th, Ste. 200
Lincoln, NE 68512
www.iuniverse.com

ISBN: 0-595-19022-7

Printed in the United States of America

The cover's design is a collection of frozen moments

Contents

Dedication

For all those who know that if life is about anything it's about trying again and again and again and again and again and again

Time is the clock of life—it chronicles and heals
balancing the euphoric with the traumatic
giving perspective to all of man's affairs
whether war childbirth, marriage/divorce, bankruptcy
earthquakes or the development of nuclear fission.
From generation to generation, it seems repetitively clear
the young waste minutes hours days even years.
Their parents—protestations to the contrary
treasure each and every moment
Once around is all you get

Life's problems do have solutions
but unfortunately no easy answers
What I have written does not pretend to be profound
prodigious or prolific
What I humbly offer is a sharing of my world
with all of you who still view the glass as half-full

J.L. Sherman Oaks California

Book I

Love & Marriage

The Good, The Bad...
And The Other Stuff

Can man ever be satisfied
Is there really such a thing as total happiness
The perfect—whatever
wife husband car house lover child
or is all of life relative
Although men and women are basically the same
as they were when in the Garden of Eden
today's Technology
has bribed them into thinking more is better
when in actuality
less is more
that's what is so refreshing about writing Aphorisms.

MARRIAGE

Is an imperfect partnership witnessed by two imperfect people
advertised to have a near perfect lifestyle
Those that succeed have partners that care enough
for what ever reasons
to hold on to what they have
rather than argue about what they don't have
Death divorce and desertion
are the only things that can dissolve it
and sometimes not even they
It's more important that **minds** match up than bodies

To do **both** takes a lifetime
A seed must be watered and cared for
before you can hold the flower in your hand
A partnership must be nurtured with love and trust
before the union can blossom

The Good Stuff

Love-is a mystery so deep that any answers
reasons or conclusions are totally illogical
Einstein was once quoted as saying that were he in love at the time
he would never have arrived at E=MC2

Love can have the destructive force of an earthquake
the quiet rapture of a mile-high trout stream
the anger of an 800 pounds gorilla
or the treasured joy of a nursing mother

When it comes—and it will—count your blessings
but be sure to hold on with both hands
For however long it lasts—generally a lifetime
it will be a roller coaster ride you won't soon forget.
It's peaks and valleys range from dancing on the moon to crying hysteri-
cally in your sleep
fearing you will never wake up...but awaken you do
to the tender lips of your nuturing partner wife mate friend
who will always be there for you

Love is forever carried in the womb of time.

Spring Love

She said "Have you waited all your life for this"
The this she was referring to was us
and the miraculous way in which we fell paralyzing in love.
Two people from dissimilar worlds waiting since childhood.
It was syllogistically true that over the years
both of us saw from time to time
something, that approximated what we each wanted
but never did we even come close to that
and now in a life span of a millisecond
we mysteriously found our dream
a friend partner and nurturer
someone who knows what it means to say
I love you
The hunger of waiting has dissolved into the joy of living

A
good
marriage
is
a
more
perfect
design
than
the
Eiffel
Tower

Love is the exhilaration of life
the goodness in being
But
when one is starved for affection
it's hard to tell love from the other stuff

All too often
the marital
seed
is planted
but never watered

The good part—Love is a two-way street
The bad part—when it turns into a one-way

Love can play terrible tricks,
the
worst
one
is
disappearing.

When
love
becomes
possessive
it
becomes
a
prison

Without love,
man will wither
and the earth
will be turned
over to the
cockroaches

Love is the ultimate in risk
It's also the ultimate in being

Happiness is sharing the same breathing
space with someone you love who loves you

Whether you are dealing with
banking or marriage
both institutions are fragile
human and dependent on
trust
for their growth and success
Should the trust stop for any
reason both would fail
Lots of them are doing just
that these days

Divorce is a lose, lose situation
Especially
for
the children who were
snatched
from their dreams

Marriage
is not a
relationship
consumed
by love
but a
collection of
loving
moments

Couples
don't need
much when
they have
each other.
Because
Fulfillment
comes in
sharing

Love has been with man
in man and of man
since creation
It nurtures the one
giving and the one
receiving
and yet so little
is shared

Some marriages
settle into a warm
cultivated soil creating
a rich nurturing bed
for the deepening roots
and future budding
while others are
strangled by the
lack of sunshine

Poverty
is not
only
being
without
money
It's
being
without
someone
to
love

Love
is the only
God-given
gift
that enables
Man
to start over
and over
and over
again

Never let your desire to be loved
exceed
your need for peace

For some
it's
easier
to make
love
than
to
offer it

Love is the
mainsail of marriage
Sacrifice
the
Tiller

Love
never enters the heart the same
way twice

I don't have to hold her in my arms
to feel the warmth of her body
the softness of her lips
the intoxication of her scent
I can do that
from a thousand miles away

Love asks that we become
a patient listener
and an unconditional
giver.
Is that asking too much
Some times

Disappointments
are woven
into the
fabric of life
Expectations are
of our making

Love not what
you are
but only
what you may
become

Cervantes

Ah how skillful grows the hand
That obeyeth Love's command
It is the heart and not the brain
That to the highest doth attain
And he who followeth Love's behest
Far excelleth all the rest

Longfellow

Love
Faith
and
Trust
are
activated
by
courage.

Love is an attack
on the heart
that's left to the
mind to sort out

Book II

Life Experiences

Those of us who remember WWII
know that today's relationships between men and women
have changed irrevocably.
From the job maker to the home to the mores of today's
society man is no longer the only force in the workplace
From the pill to the microwave from coffee to marriage
Instant is in and so are two-paycheck families.
The fact that in some cases the wife has matriculated
to the level of responsibility and earnings of the man
does give the partnership a measure of financial
security although questionable emotional stability
The working woman is succeeding in Wall Street
Hollywood, Business, Advertising, Manufacturing
Design, etc.—She has taken charge of her life
as well as bringing forth another generation
into this hostile, angry world. A role
                        that cannot be given to anyone else.

Life is like a card game.
Every twenty-four hours you're dealt a new hand and those are the only cards you can play
Tomorrow's cards may be better or
worse but you will only know that tomorrow

Innocence will eventually be tarred by
the brush of time

Flying teaches us many lessons.
One is that life has no automatic pilot

The past never dies it's
just hidden by cobwebs
So
don't dwell on it
there's no future in it

I've spent too much time walking
throught the minefields of life
not to know the sound of gunfire

Dysfunctional families
like damaged fruit
mark their own

Today lawyers and judges
have managed to play all
sorts of games with man's
reason truth and common
sense—money is the Enabler

Words are the message bearer of history

The presidential race of 2000
exposed America's greed and
the under belly of our legal system

When writing about history
hindsight is corrected vision

Writing is one
of the
most
humbling
forms of
creativity

Age is like dampness
you can't see it but
you feel it all over

We
all
cry
in
our
sleep
some times

Relationships can
become as thin as paper
and as fragile as glass
But
They are the entrees
of life. Everything else is
an after dinner mint

There are hidden costs in all of life which
can't be charged to Visa or Mastercard
regardless of how good your credit is

Human emotions are as inconsistent as life

The match of Ignorance inflames
the violence of youth

Time after time after time
we create our own hell

Today most thank yous are clichés

The emotional scars of life
can't be removed by plastic surgery

Sex sells—so does caca
if you package it properly

Talking sometimes has a
way of crumbling words like
stale bread whereas writing
connects the mind to the hand
not the tongue

Why is it that
some people always
find a way to miss
the Bus

Man is a political animal
caressed by temptation

Minds enter the world empty
what you fill them with
remains till death

Today's world wide
anger and frustration
are rubbing against
one another like
giant plates in a
seismic fault

Power

has it's own window on the World

All of us have baggage
so be sure you can carry
yours and hers up a mountain
Chiropractors and lawyers
are expensive

Be careful what you cut down in the winter
in might have flowered in the spring

Man
is served
best
by his
own voice

In penetrating the other person's Body
We
discover a knowledge of us both
and
a more open discovery of ourselves
Between
man and woman is the deepest
most
meaningful experience in life
Creation

Resurrecting
the past
is like
shaking
a mop
full of dust

The essence of creation is life
You can either learn from it or
you can fight it. You can't outlive it

Wisdom comes through pain
maturity from growth

The only time you get something etched
in stone is when you reach the cemetery

No one graduates from the classroom of life
Homework has its own reward

Differences in color are
no less human
then differences in size

So many people build walls to
protect their feelings
only to find out they
have become
a prisoner of there own emotions

Successful people tend to
drive themselves up over
and through

Time
is
not
recyclable

Life is not hooked up to a VCR
There's no fast forward or reverse

Cogito ergo sum
I think therefore I am

Rene Descartes

The older we get the more
we feel like a renter
and less like an owner

Try as you may no one
gets life on their terms

It's the Journey that counts
Birth and Death are punctuation marks

Ignorance is man's Biggest impediment

Lessons learned from pain last the longest

Gentleness is being dropped
from the lexicon of life

Book III

God & Man

Silhouetted against a gray winter's sky
are the naked limbs of a giant oak
portending a spring of unbelievable beauty
The eyes of faith see Nature's gorgeousness
as they do the newly born child

There is no such thing as the
common man
Man is
uncommonly the key to
creation

There is nothing on the outside
that can defeat what I have
on the inside—Almighty God

A priest's vestments don't make him Holy
Anymore then a judge's
Robe makes him Wise

God is the ultimate chess master
He sees a lifetime of moves

God's love gave man the gift of Co-Creation through
sharing a part of Himself with us

If God acted like man
would any of as still be here
Amazing what some of us do
in his name

Because God
hasn't
answered you
doesn't mean
He's
hard of
hearing

Man blames—God forgives
Even those who claim He doesn't exist

Love is a part of nature as nature is a part of God

Too often I find God has me
repeating a course I
thought I passed
Either God is a
tough grader or
a marvelous
teacher
I hope
the latter

The longer you live
the more you
realize that life
is really between
you
and God

Like no other Pope of this century
John XXIII
knew his flock
and his role as Shepard

Tears either interrupt
our prayers
or are an extension to them

Judgments are made by both
God and Man
but only one counts

The pristine beach's of early spring draws
attention to the ocean's rolling waves
Offering man a naked freedom that
reduces him to the barest of self.
A solitary being on a solitary
beach surrounded
by a profusion of God's gifts

No man can reverse life's cycle
and God chooses not to

We entered this world through
God's power, love
and two people who chose
to be our Mother and Father
Marital status doesn't change a biological happening
We are still a child of our Creator

There are no dress rehearsals
each day is an original
signed by God

Please God let my power
to remember only
be exceeded by my
power to forgive

We're all here
by appointment
of the king—Christ

Man can only speak of Earth
God speaks of Heaven and Earth

The pope sleeps alone
What does he know
about contraception

Forgiving means
Forgetting
One without the other is just an exercise

You can't correct yesterdays
abuses with today's Holy Water

Women come in all different shapes and sizes
but mommies are the most beautiful because
they are God's Life Bearer- even His own Son

Man is God's creation
not the other way around

Even the wisest of men
must be content
with but a fragment
of the whole truth

St. Thomas Aquinas

I came that they may have life
and have it abundantly

John 10:10

Book IV

Money & Man

The dictionary defines money as
any acceptable currency used as a
medium of exchange.
Its use will always be a double
edged sword and like truth
an individual responsibility
The banks the bankruptcies
the homeless, the jobless, the aged
the ill, the children
1 out of 8 goes to bed hungry.
The misuse of the land, and the reckless
pollution of the lakes, streams and rivers.
How can that be
We're the richest country on earth
What's happened to our medium of exchange
Is it money or man or the combination

Is it harder to make money or keep
friends you've outgrown

One is always a prisoner of his
financial debts He can also be
a prisoner of someone's kindness

A lack of money sometimes
can act as a prevention to
marriage but never to pregnancy

Sometimes repaying
one's debts is like
trying to run
away in one's
dreams

Money buys goods and services
it can also buy friendship
love and one's own children

Between friends lending money
has a perverse way of
inferring certain custodial rights

He who steals my wallet gets nothing
But he who steals my heart gets the bank

Owing money is like
not being able to go
potty by yourself

Money has both power and dignity
It all depends on who handles it

Book V

Miscellaneous

The day's cacophony of sounds
fights my emerging thoughts as
the body seeks its rest and my head
falls onto the cool pillow closing out the day
from whence comes miscellaneous

The Hollywood system
twists and turns creative
people as if they were
part of
Rubik's cube

The child inside all of us
never stops looking
for the
Rainbow

Laughter is a jolly good cuddle

Should we choose to become a **DOER,** then
forever after we must function like a turtle who
has to stick his neck out before he goes anywhere
Along with the stretched neck we're also made
aware that a **DOER** doesn't necessarily receive his
reward from his fellowman or fellow turtle He
receives it from himself for doing what he must
do rather what he wants to do

Sometimes doing nothing
is the hardest thing in the whole world

Age quietly
banks the
fires of youth

Truth is to courage
what lies are to fear

Complete trust
implies a certain
abject nakedness
But
if one really trusts
nakedness
is of little concern

Sometimes the past drags us
along the ground
like an inflated
parachute

Some need the attention of ten
rather than the love of one

Lies tend to act like a boomerang

Our time in life varies
But what doesn't vary is that
we only go around once
That is
unless you're Shirley MacLaine

Life will always be a struggle
a struggle to be born
to breathe to live—to survive
In marriage and out of marriage
with children and without
In sickness and in health
In success and failure
with money and without
But life will always be for the living
So don't try to stop the tides
hold back the winds or darken the sun
It's not yours to do

People constantly talk about
winners and losers,
never realizing that **FAILURE**
is the chisel that shapes success

Ignorance builds its own walls

I'm old enough to remember
when sex involved love and responsibility
Now it's just an exchange of bodily fluids

Pain is the half-brother of creativity

Being creative in Hollywood
is like trying to grow roses on the freeway

People who can't communicate
pray they meet a ventriloquist

Too often the smog of living blocks out
the beauty of life

Correct answers don't always provide
the most knowledge
Sometimes it takes falling on your ass

Fear
only
adds
it
can't
subtract

Whatever combat zone you enter
be sure you know the difference
between bullshit and bullets

Dreaming, gives the brain a
balloon ride

Emotional security
doesn't have
secrets
or
secret places

After birth
the only certainty one has is death
Everything in between is either unknown
or a crapshoot

No one no matter how
rich or how wise
escapes the pain of mistakes

There are three things in this world
that everyone from 3 to 130 understands
Pain Fear Love

In the biting gray cold of winter
it's impossible to smell a freshly
mowed lawn.
Or see a row of bright
spring tulips
or feel the warmth of a
summer's rain.
Pain is ever so similar

Writing brings
forth the
directness
of a child the
befuddlement
of a first kiss
and the exaltation
of a meaningful
Love
Then suddenly
everything is
muted by
an insecurity
equal to a
surgeon's initial
entrance into a
Living Brain

It's not always possible
to be a champion
but it is possible
to have
the
Heart of One

Everyone who works in the Entertainment Industry
lives in a gold fish bowl
Even when you have to go potty
At least it seems that way

Anger like grief left unresolved
can last a lifetime

Never talk about failures
they have a voice of their own

Hearing good jazz
is like meeting
a beautiful woman

Good sex can put
time on hold

Things get done and changes are made
because of one person
the rest is overkill

Two professions that need
perfect vision
Diamond cutters and Gynecologists

Talking is like water when panning for gold
Too much flushes everything away

Few things succeed like Obsession

Winston Churchill...Success is never final

What's a generation gap
It's the hole dug by the young
for the elders to fall into

Reasons are found in the present
answers in the past

Is the flesh strong or weak
It depends on whether you're
in Bed or in a Boxing Ring

Ignorance has a way of squeezing
all the good out of the Goodness

Most people talk to communicate
Others
just to ear themselves

Friendships
provide
an opportunity
to learn
more about
ourselves

Judge the sum
not the parts
of a man
painting a friend
a wife a generation

If we can have charity
towards those we
have
Loved
and lost
we can walk tall
into the sunset

For the Earth to be saved
from the ravages of ignorance
every man must be
an educator

The gurus say less is more
But not for the poor of the streets

Today's technology continues to
strip man of his privacy

You can freeze water
But you can't freeze time

Good memories
are free holidays

Any relationship not built on truth
is an accident waiting to happen

What was—is a memory
What is—is reality

Greatness finds it's own time and place

Today beauty and
money compliment one another
Ouél dommage

Physically naked is exposed truth
emotionally naked
is a
conundrum

Book VI

The older we get the faster one's life
flashes across our computer chip
setting into motion the giant relay
system that clicks through the daily
garbage codifying the important
for later review

Epilogue

Several years ago on one of my trips to England
I was, treated to a personal tour of Oxford University.
The actual tour i.e., on campus, lasted four days and then two
evenings visiting some neighborhood pubs which can best
be described as Gemütlich.
For me, the high point of the tour centered on the various
libraries, which needless to say left my limited lexicon on empty.
It was here that I was privileged to leaf through a rare collection
of Shakespeare's works, including some elaborate notes on
Man's Responsibility to Man
Man's Relationship to the Divinity
plus a small book containing an essay on
Love and Man's Link to Creation
But Creation was only one side of a two-sided treatise
The other and broader side referred to the commitment
one makes to anything He or She loves.
i.e. family, husband, brother, sister, work, church, sports, music,
art, friends, etc, etc.
So as not to be misunderstood at the end of this magnificent tribute
He synthesized His feelings in one simple sentence.
Friends He Said "Don't Fornicate Around With Love."

Shakespeare's involvement in the epilogue was a deliberate fabrication on the part of
the writer-so as to memorably implant on the mind of the reader the importance of Love.

A MEMORY

While trying to conclude my thoughts on the past years I find that I am still being drawn apprehensively to yesterday's cobwebs. Memorial day came and went this year again washing up on the sandy beaches of my mind bloody reminders of combat at seventeen and how fortunate I was to survive the winter of '44 in the Hüertgen Forest.

It was there two days after Thanksgiving, that fate tried three times to collect my dog tags. By all rights I should have been killed others were... was it a miracle a providential occurrence or a profusion of parental prayers Whatever my survival has always caused much reflective musing. I've wondered about my present lifestyle about the degree to which I have repaid my debt of life. Then too wondering as only a child can is my Father now sorry now that he saved me and not someone else? Surely He must have known that my labors in His vineyard would be flawed by my humanness. Is it just me who expected more or did He as well

The reality of life is that we have one alpha and one omega. There are no exceptions, not even for His only son. If the years haven't been kind they have been enlightening. Then too, age has played a constructive part in establishing a better balance and deeper understanding enabling all that's inside of me to hum like my Accutron watch.

Ergo, I will continue to make as many constructive changes as He gives me time to make. A.M..D.G.

On the 16th day of Nov. 2000 I was awarded the Bronze Star and a Presidential Unit Emblem for Northern France and the Rhineland.

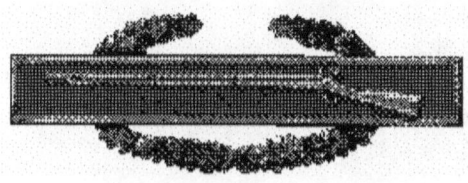

School Days

**Some friends who have
left their finger prints
on my heart.**

Donald Mc Conville, Bro. Daniel F. Curtin, George T. Bacon Jr. Bridget Gaffney, Ella Chivis, Eno & Loretta De Pasquale, Eric & Ella Turner, Ed Desnoes, Mae A. Lemle, Victor Anderson, Ruth Gordon, Bill & Kay Tully, Gordon & Bridget O'Neill, Jim Kerin, Ken & Susie Turner, Eno & Kay De Pasquale Jr, Bill & Margaret Wilkinson Capt James Stark, (My Sons) Peter & Jim, Noelle Seberle, Hank & Sally Lichtman, Jack & Gloria Kramer, Ted & Ann Schroeder, Pancho & Beverly Segura, Fr. Thomas Killackey, Fr. Ray Sullivan,Buzz Kulik, Jeanne Harrison, Bob Kronenberg, Helen Mc Arthur, Ev Hart, Diana Fisher, Dick Kerns, Dr. Edward Miller, John & Thelma Rost, Julian Bercovici, Dr. Robert Abraham, Derry Moore, Bart & Joan Swift, Arnold & Wally Lavin, Mabel Wood, Alathena Smith, The Pocker Family, Rae & Doris Chisholm, Fr. Henry Johnson, Penny Buckland, Dibs and Dottie Davis, David Walsh, Msgr. Cyril Navin, Phillip Lambro, Maurice Bolotin, Harriett Bara, Wm A Fraker, Thomas Cooney, Bill & Karen Fraker IV, John Spence, Keith Sillett, Richard Hughes, Betty Fraker, Dick Colean, The man-son-hing Family, Michael Burns, Morris & Joy West, Mike Jones, Doug McLaury, Will Fitzgerald.

Harry & Nan Lichtman...Who gave me their heart.

There is more love in giving than in Having

About the Author

TV Writer, Producer, Director

Photograph by Derry Moore

All of us who deal with life head on, must accept the inevitability of pain and the reality that rewards are few and fleeting. A lot of life is about time and change, so we must move on to do what we do, because that's the way we were made.

www.ingramcontent.com/pod-product-compliance
Lightning Source LLC
Chambersburg PA
CBHW021602280526
45784CB00001BA/458